Original title:
Ferns and Feelings

Copyright © 2025 Creative Arts Management OÜ
All rights reserved.

Author: Helena Marchant
ISBN HARDBACK: 978-1-80581-744-4
ISBN PAPERBACK: 978-1-80581-271-5
ISBN EBOOK: 978-1-80581-744-4

## A Tangle of Memories Underneath the Canopy

In the shade where shadows dance,
Laughter ponders, takes a chance.
A leaf slips down with playful grace,
I trip on roots, a wild embrace.

Whispers float on summer's breeze,
Silly secrets, such a tease.
Beneath the green, we hide and seek,
Tickled giggles, bright and cheek.

A wrinkled map for where I've strolled,
Each twist and turn, a tale retold.
A squirrel scolds with lofty pride,
As I tumble, giggling wide.

The sun peeks through a leafy veil,
With every turn, we laugh, we fail.
Memories twirl like autumn's leaves,
In this jungle, joy deceives.

## The Quiet Pulse of Nature's Heart

In the woods where shadows dance,
The leaves all gossip, take a chance.
They chuckle soft as breezes blow,
In secret hues, they steal the show.

A squirrel winks, a bird will sing,
Together they form the oddest fling.
The trees, they jest, in rustling tone,
With roots that twist like they have grown.

## Lifting Up the Wistful Fronds

A jolly breeze lifts leafy hats,
The ferns are dancing, what of that?
They twirl and sway in silly glee,
Unruly greens, as wild as can be.

With every step, the ground will shiver,
Their antics make the sunlight quiver.
They giggle softly, just like kids,
In nature's play, there are no bids.

## Fern-touched Whispers of Longing

In corners quiet, secrets creep,
The ferns hold whispers, soft and deep.
They stretch and sigh with gentle grace,
In this wild world, they find their place.

Each sigh they offer has a pun,
Their humor shines like morning sun.
They tickle dew upon the ground,
With every rustle, joy is found.

## Capturing the Essence of Breath and Leaf

Among the greens, where mischief lies,
A leafy prank can catch your eyes.
They leap with joy in sunlight's glance,
Inviting anyone to dance.

The whispers here are quite absurd,
Like jesters cloaked in emerald bird.
In every crease, a story spun,
Amongst the nature, we have fun.

## Sentiments Hidden in the Lattice

In the garden, secrets grow,
Whispers dance where soft winds blow.
Leaves giggle in the dappled light,
Gossiping greens, oh what a sight!

Beneath the shade, laughter hides,
While buzzing bugs take joyrides.
Roots are plotting, deep in play,
Stirring mischief every day!

**Unfurling a Tapestry of Thoughts**

Each frond unfurls with quirky flair,
High hopes tangled in moist air.
Spindly tendrils reach for the sun,
A leafy chase just for fun!

In breezes soft, jokes take flight,
Tickling leaves with sheer delight.
Nature's giggle fills the space,
A green parade at a merry pace!

## The Delicate Interlace of Nature's Heart

Amidst the greens, a jester grows,
With playful antics, nature shows.
Twisting vines in a cheeky dance,
Inviting critters to take a chance!

A dandelion makes a wish,
Serenade with every swish.
In this patch of velvet dreams,
Even the grass giggles, it seems!

### Love Letters Written in Chlorophyll

In the foliage, love notes hide,
Written in whispers by nature's side.
Crickets chirp their sweet debates,
Producing smiles, opening gates!

Lush pages turn on a breezy day,
With every flutter, they sway and play.
It's a tale of joy, a leafy jest,
Where all are welcome, feel their best!

**Serenity Among the Fronds**

In the forest, whispers tease,
Fronds giggle in the gentle breeze.
A squirrel trips, what a sight!
He blames it on the leafy light.

Sunlight dances on green lace,
Mossy beds invite a race.
In the shade, the laughter grows,
As everyone's stepping on their toes.

## The Unseen Dance of the Woodland

Things shuffle softly under leaves,
A fox in glasses, what a tease!
With a hat made of a clover crown,
He tips it well before falling down.

The trees sway as if they know,
Every secret joke in tow.
As branches chuckle, shadows prance,
They join the forest's wild dance.

## Shadows in the Understory

In the dark, a bunny hops,
Ties its shoes and then it stops.
A raccoon giggles, 'Don't be shy!
Let's hula-hoop, just you and I!'

Mushrooms stand in timeless stare,
As if to say, 'Life's not unfair!'
Each cap wears a patch of glee,
Dancing dreamers, wild and free.

## Growth Between the Roots

Underneath the twisted ground,
Little sprouts are gathering round.
Whispers swirl of organic cheer,
Who knew that worms could persevere?

With a wiggle, roots entwine,
Sharing secrets over wine.
A giggle slips from sleepy grass,
'Did you hear that? Time to pass!'

## Nature's Silent Soliloquy

In the garden where giggles grow,
Leaves dance wildly, putting on a show.
With whispers of laughter on gentle air,
The blooms chuckle softly, without a care.

The beetles are busy, gossiping low,
While butterflies flutter, stealing the glow.
Every petal has secrets, bright and quaint,
As squirrels plot mischief, no trace of restraint.

## **Tangles of Tenderness**

A rabbit hops with a leap and a bound,
Searching for snacks that are scattered around.
The daisies tease him, swaying in tease,
As he sneezes loudly, bringing them to knees.

Oh, the vines twist and tangle with glee,
Snapping photos with a giddy decree.
The wisdom of shrubs, comical and wise,
Makes even the hedgehog crack silly lies.

## **Gossamer Dreams of the Forest**

In a dreamland of dappled sunlight's caress,
The spiders are busy, creating their mess.
Webs shimmer with giggles, as if they conspire,
To catch all the chuckles, the whimsy they admire.

Birds chirp sonnets, a lark's rendition,
While ants hold a party, with great ambition.
Dancing on petals, there's joy in the fray,
Nature's a jester, making all come play.

## The Sway of Silent Spirits


Trees whisper riddles in arms that entwine,
As shadows play tag in a dance that's divine.
Mushrooms wear hats that are far too grand,
While the foxes just giggle, making life planned.

The sun winks down, with a mischievous grin,
As clouds throw shade, spurring laughter within.
A critter's parade in the vibrant delight,
Nature throws parties, till the fall of night.

## Thoughts among the Thickets

In a green patch, I ponder so,
A squirrel winks, should I say hello?
The leaves dance gently, whispering tales,
Of bugs with dreams and tiny snails.

A plant with style, it roots in place,
Daring to grow, it wins the race.
I trip on a vine, give a chuckle loud,
As a butterfly lands, looking so proud.

With shadows playing trickster's game,
Each step I take, feels a bit lame.
Yet nature laughs, all beneath the sun,
In thickets where every day's a pun.

So join this dance, all soft and green,
In the wild where giggles are seen.
Let laughter sprout like flowers so bright,
In the thickets where joy takes flight.

## The Cool Embrace of the Earth

Laying down on a patch of moss,
Feeling quite noble, like a boss.
The world spins fast, but here I sway,
Befriending the bugs that come out to play.

A rock rolls by, with style and flair,
It tips its hat, what a charming affair!
I shout out loud, 'You're looking fine!'
It winks back—oh, a clever line!

Tickling breezes tease my hair,
While toads croak songs, they sing with flair.
The soil beneath holds secrets deep,
Where laughter and dreams play hide and seek.

In this embrace, I'm free and bold,
With stories whispered, yet to be told.
So lie with me, in chill and cheer,
Amongst earth's wonders, let's disappear.

## Hidden Emotions in the Foliage

Behind each leaf, a secret dwells,
Got my heart tangled in endless swells.
The weeds gossip low with mischievous glee,
While the daisies roll their eyes at me.

So many feelings trapped in green,
A tangled mess, if you know what I mean!
The wind giggles, shaking the trees,
Whispering tales of silliness with ease.

A lonesome branch waves, "Come take a chance!"
While spiders spin out a web of romance.
Plant pals tease about love so sly,
'It's stickier than sap, oh my, oh my!'

Beneath the canopy, emotions play,
In this grassy theater, come what may.
Join the circus where laughter is grand,
Hidden surprises at every hand.

## Beneath the Fronded Veil

A shady nook where giggles grow,
Under the leaves, it's quite the show.
Spaces where chatter happens fast,
With vines that twist and laughter cast.

The breeze carries tales from far away,
Of critters who dance and frolic all day.
Each frond a whisper, each leaf a grin,
Creating mischief, let the fun begin!

Mossy stools for the weary and wise,
As ants march by, in grand disguise.
In this green world, we're all a bit weird,
Embracing quirks, never feared.

So come join in the jolly spree,
Where the fronds know all, just wait and see.
Beneath the veil, the friendship's true,
In our leafy realm, there's room for you!

## The Intricacies of Light and Sentiment

In the dappled glade, shadows skip,
Chuckling softly, they never trip.
Sunbeams dance like clumsy sprites,
Chasing giggles, lost to heights.

A squirrel snickers, wearing shades,
As laughter echoes, nature parades.
Leaves flutter like gossiping friends,
Tickled by breezes, that never ends.

The sun winks down, a cheeky tease,
Rustling jokes among the trees.
Nature's humor, wild and free,
Where every leaf's a joke, you see!

Amid the chaos, joy abounds,
Time rolls over, without bounds.
In this realm, where whimsy plays,
Life's a jester, in leafy displays.

## Fern-taught Lessons in Stillness

In corners where the green things grow,
Wisdom whispers soft and low.
A leaf giggles with a grin,
Teaching patience from within.

With each rustle, life unfolds,
Stories of laughter, brave and bold.
Nature points to amusing quirks,
To find the fun where stillness lurks.

Beneath the shade of ancient trees,
Jokes are carried on the breeze.
They tell of times when hearts were light,
As shadows dance into the night.

In calmness found, a chuckle lies,
As critters plot their next surprise.
Stillness here is never bland,
With playful joy at hand in hand.

## **A Garden of Untold Stories**

In the garden, secrets play,
Beneath the green, they sway and say.
Petals giggle, seeds plot mischief,
Whispering tales of dreams, so brief.

Bumblebees buzz in merry tune,
While ladybugs dance beneath the moon.
Flora grins with cheeky glee,
Sprinkling humor like confetti.

A cat stumbles, chasing a breeze,
Dandling leaves, hoping to tease.
Nature's pranks bloom all around,
In this wild, laughing, leafy ground.

From roots to tips, the fun unwinds,
It's all a game, if one just finds.
Untold stories, in green confide,
Escaping laughter, they can't abide.

**Emotions Wrapped in Green**

Wrapped in shades of vibrant hue,
Feelings giggle, fresh and new.
In the thicket, laughter sways,
Making joy in playful ways.

A rabbit bows with a honked nose,
Tickling tufts where laughter grows.
Whispers rustle like soft sighs,
Each one cloaked in merry lies.

The wind plays tricks, in tangled vines,
As humor flutters like a thousand pines.
Sunlight sprinkles, the warmth it brings,
In the garden of leafy things.

So come and see, where fun resides,
Where giggles grow, and joy abides.
In every nook, the green's been seen,
The world is silly, wrapped in green!

## Moss-Covered Memories

In a forest where shadows play,
Lively whispers brighten the day.
A squirrel scurries, cheeky and bold,
Stealing acorns, a sight to behold.

Moss coats the rocks with soft green fluff,
While wily rabbits start acting tough.
They hop and they skip with comical style,
Making the grumpy badger smile.

The trees hold secrets, tales untold,
Of laughing leaves, both timid and old.
With every rustle, a tickle of cheer,
The forest invites us to linger here.

Sunlight dances on soft, bristled grounds,
Nature's laughter fills all the sounds.
And everything grows, quite reckless and wild,
Even the squirrels, they're nature's own child.

## Heartbeats in the Hush

Amidst the calm, a buzz breaks through,
A gopher sneezes, 'Achoo, a-choo!'
The echoes ripple across the glen,
Startling deer, and then they sprint again.

Murmurs of joy play hide-and-seek,
As frogs croak softly, their voices unique.
A ladybug dangles, defying the breeze,
With poses so silly, if only you please!

The brook gurgles tales of foolish fish,
Who wiggle and giggle, what a strange wish!
Cactus pricks tickle, barely a scare,
When prancing past blooms, who knew they're there?

Every hush hides a grin, wild and free,
In this woodland treat, come dance with me.
Breathe in the joy, let laughter unroll,
For heartbeats in stillness can utterly bowl!

## **Silhouettes of Serenity**

In the twilight, shadows take flight,
A cat's rude meow gives a gentle fright.
Bumblebees stumble, their dance an art,
Whirling around—a nature's mishart.

Tall weeds wave like they're making a scene,
As a bold raccoon steals a cucumber green.
They bask in the glow of the dusk's sweet light,
Where every misstep feels just so right.

Branches stretch out with a weary sigh,
Contemplating dreams as the night drifts by.
A snail slides past, slow winner indeed,
While the fireflies twinkle, following speed.

Hoots from nearby hint at a game,
A fox plays hide-and-seek, wild and untame.
With silhouettes swaying against the night's edge,
Laughter echoes upon nature's ledge.

## Gentle Caress of the Wilderness

The breeze twirls softly, like a playful friend,
Whispering secrets that never quite end.
Thorns take a bow, they're part of the cast,
While daisies chuckle; this fun's unsurpassed.

Butterflies giggle in colors so bright,
While the owls mumble, 'Is it day or night?'
A raccoon drops berries with clumsiness grand,
While squirrels throw shade on their fruit-filled stand.

Pinecones roll down with a tinkling sound,
As the river chuckles, its joy all around.
Each splash is a jest, a giddy old jest,
Where nature can laugh, and truly, it's best.

In this green canopy, grin wide and loud,
Let the wonder within you feel hefty and proud.
For wildness and whimsy join hand in hand,
A gentle embrace of this splendid land.

## Whispers of the Woodland

In the glade where laughter grows,
A tickle from the leaves bestows.
The critters dance, all in a row,
While mushrooms giggle, 'Oh, let's go!'

A wily squirrel with nuts to share,
Sings a song that fills the air.
With every bounce, he shakes his tail,
As if to say, 'Oh, here's my trail!'

The sun peeks through, the shadows play,
Each branch a jest, brightening the day.
A rabbit snorts, a bad joke told,
While daisies burst with laughter bold.

So come and join this woodland spree,
Where woodland spirits dance with glee.
And amidst the fun and light-hearted cheer,
You'll find your worries disappear!

## Echoes in the Underbrush

In the depths where secret giggles teem,
The bushes throb with a happy dream.
Little insects host a parade,
While poor old foxes, they're dismayed.

'Why so downcast?' a ladybug said,
'Join the party, clear your head!'
With fluttering wings and dizzy spins,
They dive into a dance, grins to grins.

Frogs in tuxedos croak a tune,
And crickets strum beneath the moon.
The crowd's a riot, such joyous brash,
As fireflies flash like a disco bash.

So let the whispers guide your way,
Through laughter-infused, leafy fray.
With each soft rustle, they tease and poke,
Creating warm, delightful jokes.

## **Fern Fronds and Heartstrings**

Green fans waving, oh what a sight,
They flirt with breezes, a true delight.
In this cozy nook, mere laughter reigns,
Even the shadows play little games.

A cheeky gnome on a mushroom thrones,
Making sweet music with squeaky tones.
'Hey, you ferns, come sway with me!'
The howls of laughter, oh, can't you see?

The wind whispers jokes, all in good fun,
As petals giggle in the warming sun.
The roots below tap in a wild beat,
While the dew drops chant, 'Life is sweet!'

So let's twirl 'round, let joy unfurl,
Dance with the blades in this magical whirl.
With each turn, we'll share our cheer,
In this delightful forest sphere.

## Shadows Beneath the Canopy

Beneath the trees, where shadows twirl,
The forest hosts a fancy whirl.
With every rustle, joy ignites,
As owls in tuxedos throw wild nights.

'What's that? A joke?' a raccoon inquires,
As bonfire spirits play with lighters.
A squirrel jokes, 'I lost a bet,
Now I'm stuck here, owe my debt!'

Dancing mushrooms break out in song,
Each note a chuckle, it won't be long.
The ferns all shimmy, what a crowd!
Together they cheer, oh, life's so loud!

So roam through shadows, take part in fun,
Where the whispers combine 'til day is done.
In this playful glade, laughter shines bright,
Embrace the humor 'neath the moonlight.

## Soft Fern Fronds and Tender Thoughts

In the garden, fronds do sway,
Tickling toes, come out to play.
Whispers of joy in the spring air,
Nature's giggles everywhere!

Silly greens dance with delight,
Catch the sun, almost a sight!
They hide the bugs, oh what a treat,
Making picnic days so sweet!

Leaves in hats, oh what a view,
Breezy jokes just waiting for you.
In petals' laughter, all is bright,
We grin and poke in pure delight!

Frolicking under skies so blue,
Each sprout spins tales, so funny too.
In this patch, all woes depart,
A leafy party, straight from the heart!

**Nature's Gentle Caress**

A tickle on the arm, a breeze,
Whispering secrets through the trees.
Nature's hugs, softly on my skin,
Turning frowns to silly grins!

The daisies wink, they start to tease,
Swaying together with the leaves.
Each breeze carries a chuckle behind,
A garden comedy, perfectly timed!

Overhead, the clouds do laugh,
Taking selfies with the grass.
Sunshine sparkles, a radiant show,
In this playful, vibrant glow!

With every fern a funny pose,
Nature, in jest, always knows.
Catching joy, tucked here and there,
A chuckle shared everywhere!

## **Ferns in the Twilight of Emotion**

As day gives way to starlit skies,
Frogs croon their songs, oh what a surprise!
Shadows blend, and giggles rise,
Nature's jest hidden in disguise.

Moonlit paths invite a dance,
Twisting and turning, give it a chance.
Whimsical whispers from dusk till dawn,
Every leaf sings, until you yawn!

With creeping vines, slyly they weave,
Tales of the heart, do you believe?
In the twilight, secrets are spun,
Nature's joke, we're all just one!

Up above, the stars do wink,
Dancing lanterns make us think.
In this realm of nighttime glee,
The world's a stage, so wild and free!

## Secrets of the Underbrush

Under thickets, creatures play,
Mischievous shadows lead the way.
Squirrels gossip, no time to waste,
Life's a joke, with laughter laced!

Leaves rustle with a comic flair,
Tickled by wind, they dance in air.
Grumpy hedgehogs hold their ground,
While silly ants race all around!

Tangled vines share stories bold,
Of childish hearts and dreams retold.
Every nook holds laughter's song,
In the underbrush, we all belong!

Hidden gems and chuckles abound,
In nature's heart, joy knows no bounds.
Here in the thicket, fun's the rule,
A leafy laughter, nature's school!

## Twirling Memories under Lush Canopies

In the dance of leaves we prance,
Each twist a giggle, a playful chance,
Squirrels stare as we curtsy low,
They whisper, 'A comedy show!'

The sun peeks through with a sly grin,
Tickling our toes as we spin,
A breeze joins in, so bold and brash,
We laugh hard, avoiding the splash.

A bird joins the fun, sings a tune,
Accidental notes, a buffoon's swoon,
With roots entwined, we plot our spree,
Joking 'round the trunk of a giddy tree.

At dusk, we collapse under starlit hue,
Recalling the moments, feeling anew,
In nature's arms, let laughter abound,
For joy, we've found, is all around.

## Nature's Dialogues with the Heart

Whispers flutter on the wind's breath,
Bantering blooms with a hint of jest,
A ladybug rolls like a tumbleweed,
As pine cones joke, oh yes indeed!

The river giggles, it starts to bubble,
Frogs join the chorus, creating trouble,
Leaves tickle each other, a leafy fight,
Nature's chatters, a silly delight.

In the shadow of moss, we'd rest and sigh,
Listening in on the babbling sky,
Clouds chase each other, so light and free,
Saying, 'You can't catch what you can't see!'

At dusk, we bask in warmth and cheer,
Nature's humor, forever dear,
As the stars wink down in a playful array,
We chuckle at all that's gone astray.

## Secrets Span the Forest Lattice

Beneath the canopy, secrets thrive,
A chipmunk's wink, where mischiefs arrive,
Laughter echoes through the twisted vines,
As nature plays on invisible lines.

Eavesdropping on the blooms' sweet chatter,
Each petal whispers what really matters,
They tease the sunlight, 'Come join our game,'
Nature's gossip, never quite the same.

Among the roots, tales intertwine,
A thousand stories in weathered design,
With each rustle, jests are spread,
'Who needs a bed? Just use the thread!'

At twilight's call, we share a giggle,
In leafy corners, our hearts wiggle,
For every secret from the bark and bough,
Nature's laughter is with us now.

## Shades of Longing in the Quiet Grove

In the quiet wood where shadows play,
A whimsy beckons the light of day,
Wanderers stumble on roots like jokes,
As laughter bursts from giggling oaks.

Mushrooms blush under tales of old,
They whisper further than they're told,
Each squirrel plots with a devilish grin,
Snatching snacks while we just grin.

The wind carries stories both merry and shy,
As dandelions dance, waving goodbye,
In this lush nook, we bask and delight,
In chuckles shared as stars ignite.

With every rustle, a hearty laugh,
Nature's twist on the seasonal path,
As dusk falls gently, we find our place,
In the grove's humor, we find our grace.

## Beneath the Surface of Solitude

Lurking beneath the leafy veil,
A squirrel tells a bizarre tale.
Of acorns lost and nuts gone rogue,
While raccoons sway in happy vogue.

Mossy whispers tickle the ground,
As laughter's echo can be found.
In shadows soft, the critters play,
Timing jokes in their own way.

A turtle grins without a care,
In his slow dance, a messy flair.
The sun peeks through in playful beams,
Tickling the plants and all their dreams.

With giggles bright, the ferns do sway,
While nature blooms in a grand ballet.
Who knew that solitude could jest?
In secret gardens, we are truly blessed.

## Fronds of Hope in the Shade

Under canopies so rich and lush,
The critters come in a happy hush.
With fronds that wave like hands in glee,
They celebrate their wild spree.

Chubby rabbits hop in a dance,
While hedgehogs glare, not taking a chance.
In tangled roots, a party brews,
Filled with laughter, odd interviews.

A wise old slug claims he's a sage,
Sharing wisdom, a slimy page.
He speaks of woes and joys anew,
While fireflies blink in the evening dew.

In shadows deep, a jester plays,
While friends unite in silly ways.
The shade becomes a stage for cheer,
In nature's bar where all draw near.

## The Debris of Dreams on Forest Floors


Beneath the leaves, a treasure hunt,
With pine cone crowns and acorn fronts.
The squirrels giggle, a raucous crew,
Building castles with sticks and dew.

In every corner, a tale's been spun,
Of mischief wrought under the sun.
Bugs dance wildly, on one leg they stand,
Holding a dance-off, impromptu and grand.

With twigs for swords, they fight their fears,
While laughter rings, the forest cheers.
In tangled mess, hilarity brews,
Each moment shared, a joyful muse.

Dreams scatter like leaves in the breeze,
With every chuckle, we find our ease.
In this forest, a playground lies,
Where every grin sparks a sweet surprise.

## Soft Green Thoughts in the Waking Woods

As dawn breaks softly on gentle streams,
The woods awaken, igniting dreams.
Frogs croak jokes, it's quite a scene,
While dragonflies dance, all gleam and sheen.

The mossy floor's a comfy bed,
Where rabbits nap, resting their heads.
With every stretch, they dream of snacks,
In this realm, we surely relax.

A chipmunk grins, his cheeks bulge wide,
Hoarding smiles like a joyful ride.
In leafy boughs, the laughter soars,
As playful minds find open doors.

With every rustle, a giggle's near,
While nature sways, we shed our fear.
In waking woods, the spirit sings,
With soft green thoughts, we find our wings.

**Ties of Earth and Emotion**

In the woods where giggles grow,
Roots of laughter start to show.
Leaves tickle toes in playful glee,
Waving 'hello' like a friendly tree.

Mossy hats on squirrels' heads,
Dance with joy upon their beds.
Bouncing limbs in syncopated rhythm,
Nature's jesters, without a schism.

Whispers of breeze, a funny sound,
Chasing shadows all around.
Grumpy toads in polka dots,
Bark like dogs in funny spots.

So here we laugh, let spirits lift,
In this place, the greatest gift.
Laughter blooms like petals wild,
In the heart of every child.

## The Lattice of Thoughts Hidden in Green

In a tangle where minds entwine,
Greens and giggles start to shine.
Curly fronds like curious cats,
Peeking shyly through the spats.

Ideas bounce like playful squirrels,
In nutty minds, they whirl and twirl.
Shadows chase the laughter here,
While bushes gossip, "What's the cheer?"

Twisting paths that tickle toes,
And wiggle grass where sunshine glows.
Lost in thought, then burst with glee,
Nature's chat is wild and free.

Laughter drips from every leaf,
A funny tale, a joyous brief.
In this maze of green delight,
Thoughts take flight in pure sunlight.

## Fragments of Joy Amongst the Leaves

Bits of laughter float like seeds,
Tickling earth with silly deeds.
A sprout of giggles here and there,
A dance of joy in the crisp air.

Caterpillars wearing silly hats,
Wiggle and squirm like playful brats.
Even the snails wear grins so wide,
As they slide down the mossy slide.

Crickets chirp a comic tune,
Underneath the laughing moon.
Every rustling leaf a tease,
Making fun of swaying bees.

In the patches where smiles grow,
Each little twist begins to show.
Joy is stitched in every seam,
Amongst the leaves, we chase a dream.

## Serenade of Shadows in the Glade

In the glade where shadows play,
Laughter twirls and runs away.
Pixies giggle behind the trees,
Making mischief with the breeze.

Frogs in crowns serenade the night,
With silly songs, they're quite a sight.
Whimsical whispers through the ferns,
In secret places where joy returns.

A raccoon waltzes on the stage,
Waving its paws, a furry mage.
Chasing shadows, what a show,
In this realm, there's never woe.

So when you find your heart at play,
Join the laughter, don't delay.
For in this glade of endless cheer,
Every little joy draws near.

## The Unfurling of the Heart

In the garden of giggles, we play,
Leaves twist like dancers in disarray.
A sprout with a shrug and a cheerful squeak,
Whispers to daisies, 'A laugh is the peak.'

With each turn and twist, joy must be shared,
Bouncing about in a world unprepared.
Nature's confetti, it sprinkles the air,
While worms tell their jokes, no one can compare.

The sun beams down, it's a silly parade,
Branches wave hands like they're making a trade.
A tickle from grass brings a chuckle and cheer,
In this leafy realm, it's always sincere.

So come join the fun, let your worries go,
In this tangled laughter, let happiness grow.
A heart on a leaf, oh the humor is bold,
In this wild theater, life's stories unfold.

## The Velvet Touch of the Glade

In the soft hush of green, there's a chuckle and sway,
Moss cushions the feet like a funny ballet.
A snail wears a hat, what a curious sight,
He's got the best jokes, it's a slippery night.

Butterflies gossip about secretive plans,
While crickets compose with their tiny bandstands.
The wind joins the chorus with a whoop and a whistle,
Even the shadows start to dance and to twizzle.

A raindrop tumbles, it lands on a frog,
And he croaks out a punchline, completing the fog.
The trees laugh along, swaying side to side,
Nature's a comedian— no place left to hide.

So come take a stroll through this glen full of cheer,
And let out a giggle, let loose with good cheer.
For in this green haven, laughter's the creed,
With the velvet of nature planting the seed.

## Whispers of the Wild

In the wild wonder, where the oddball thrives,
Bunnies wear spectacles to read and devise.
The hedgehogs are chatting, sipping their tea,
While the owls throw a party, come join, won't you see?

A squirrel with hiccups bounces through trees,
Hiding his snacks with such comical ease.
The flowers blow kisses, their petals all bright,
While the grass tickles toes in the softening light.

Foxes tell tales with a sly little grin,
About days filled with antics and laughing within.
The brook gives a giggle as it flows on its way,
Making trouble for frogs who just want to play.

So dance in the wild, hear the whispers so close,
Where every creature is bound to propose.
A life full of humor, let your heart dwell,
In this crazy patchwork where laughter must swell.

## **Veils of Verdancy**

Under leafy canopies, secrets unfurl,
A worm in a tuxedo gives quite the whirl.
The lilies are giggling, it's quite the affair,
While crickets wear ties as they twirl in midair.

In this lush little world, every plant plays a role,
With vines draping veils, they're on a rock 'n' roll stroll.
A dandelion puff joins the rhythmic delight,
Spreading wishes and laughter throughout the night.

The sunbeams are laughing, they peek through the trees,
While bushes hold parties with snacks and good cheese.
With each rustling leaf, there's a snicker or two,
In this secretive realm, pure joy comes in view.

So wander with mirth through this soft, verdant sea,
Where laughter is woven with nature's decree.
For in veils of green, the heart finds a spark,
As whimsy and wonder dance into the dark.

## The Rustling of Affection in the Brush

In the woods where giggles hide,
Little critters take a ride.
A leaf does tickle, then it twirls,
While shy roots gossip, shake, and swirl.

A badger winks, the squirrel does grin,
As whispers fade, let the fun begin.
The hedgehog dons a party hat,
With a dance-off, oh, imagine that!

Sunbeams play tag with the cool breeze,
As shadows dance among the trees.
Laughter echoes from nook to nook,
While the wise old owl just learns to cook.

The scene unfolds, wild and free,
In nature's realm, it's jubilee!
So join the fun and make a fuss,
In leafy realms, it's all of us!

## Whispers Beneath the Great Green Canopy

Beneath the leaves, a secret babbles,
Chirps and tickles, giggles and scrabbles.
The chubby worms wiggle to the beat,
While ants create a bustling street.

The sunlight peeks with a sly grin,
As frogs croak jokes, they always win.
A bunny hops with a cheeky show,
While mushrooms chuckle, row by row.

Dancing shadows join the spree,
Spinning tales of carefree glee.
The fox throws in a snarky quip,
And even the mushrooms start to flip!

Nature's laughter fills the air,
In leafy depths without a care.
So let us sip from this delight,
And giggle beneath the stars tonight!

## A Dance of Shadows and Soft Leaves

In the glen where the wild things sway,
Leaves beckon for a playful play.
The shadows chuckle in a jest,
While flowers do a fancy dress.

A shy fox pirouettes with flair,
As petals twirl without a care.
See the beetles form a train,
While mushrooms clap, who feels no pain!

Laughter swells with breezy cheer,
Tiny creatures gather near.
A squirrel spins, the dance begins,
Where laughter lives, just bustling wins.

In the rhythm of nature's jest,
Playful moments are the best.
Join the merry, let's prance and tease,
Under shadows, we find our ease!

## Signals of Nature in the Thickets

In tangled tricks, the whispers flow,
From twigs and leaves, they start to show.
The bee's a comedian, buzzing bright,
While crickets chirp in sheer delight.

A porcupine's joke strikes just the right pin,
As chubby raccoons dive right in.
The ferns nod with a secret grin,
While fireflies giggle with their spin.

Nature's signal, bold and free,
Creates a wondrous jubilee.
Soft grass giggles, nothing to lose,
As joy pops like morning hues.

In hidden realms where the wild things play,
Nature's punchlines bright the day.
So swing along, with heart on sleeve,
In wild thickets, there's joy to weave!

## The Dance of the Delicate Leaves

In the garden, they prance, so spry,
With whispers of laughs, a leafy high.
Twisting and twirling, a green ballet,
They giggle in sunlight, come out to play.

Breezes tickle, oh what a sight,
Bouncing up close, they take flight.
Chasing each other, they wear a grin,
Flapping around, let the fun begin!

Under the moon, they sway and sway,
Making the shadows at night feel gay.
With chortles and chirps, they tease the night,
A leafy affair, what a jovial delight!

So dance, little leaves, with sheer glee,
For joy is abundant, as clear as can be.
In laughter's embrace, let us all weave,
The tune of the forest, come join the reprieve.

## Ink and Ivy

Dripping with color, bees buzz with glee,
Splashing the world with a giggly spree.
Scribbles of green on a canvas so wide,
Making mischief with every glide.

Tentacles stretching, they tickle the air,
With a wink and a nod, they don't have a care.
Jokes of the earth, they're chuckling loud,
The scribbled vines, oh, so proud!

Cleverly curling, they twist with flair,
Sketching the moments, a merry affair.
Bounding along with a playful flip,
Penning the day, on a joyful trip!

Under the starlight, they giggle and gleam,
Creating a whimsy like some wild dream.
So let laughter flow through each leafy embrace,
Inking our hearts with a playful grace.

## **Mirth in the Meadow's Mist**

In the morning mist, they chatter and play,
Whispering secrets in a funny way.
Poking their heads, just two leaves on a spree,
Sharing old jokes, giggling with glee.

A squirrel scampers, they all hold their breath,
When he trips on a root, it's a moment of heft!
Laughter erupts from the greenery all,
Nature's own comedy, a splendid free-for-all!

Sunbeams shimmer, tickling each face,
They frolic and tumble in this joyous place.
With each gentle rustle, a joke to retell,
In the meadow's embrace, all is well.

As twilight descends and the day takes its bow,
The chuckles continue, with a take-a-bow.
In the soft evening, they find such bliss,
Sharing their laughter, in a world full of mist.

## Verdant Reveries

In dreams of green, they dance in delight,
Drawing the sun in a whirlwind of light.
Swaying and playing, oh what a scene,
These little green dreams, bright and serene!

With a poke and a prod, they play peek-a-boo,
They twist and they tangle, a whimsical crew.
Whispering murmurs as breezes do blow,
Tickling the fancies of all down below.

Each fluttering leaf tells a story so grand,
Of tickles and giggles in this leafy land.
They dream of the world in their frolicsome dance,
Sprinkling joy, like seeds with a chance!

So let's all join in the verdant jamboree,
With chuckles and smiles, just you and me.
In the rooty embrace, let's all take a stand,
For laughter and joy, oh isn't it grand?

## Murmurs of Green in the Soul's Depth

In the glade, a whisper sings,
Leaves gossip as the sunlight clings.
A twist of roots with a wink and grin,
Nature laughs where the heart begins.

Squishy shoes on a muddy trail,
Dancing feet tell a wobbly tale.
The breeze tickles, oh what a tease,
While squirrels plot mischief in the trees.

Joyful spores, in chaos they sprout,
While shy moss pens an awkward shout.
Giggles of petals burst into cheer,
As the world spins in its leafy sphere.

## The Fragile Balance of Heart and Nature

In the park, the grass has flair,
As butterflies float, without a care.
A dandelion whispers a dare,
While bees practice their best air fair.

Watch out! Here comes the shakey sprout,
A clumsy dance with a butterfly pout.
Leafy faces, tales so absurd,
Talk of the day when the goat stole a bird.

The root's grand party, what a sight!
Even the earthworms dress up so bright.
A giggle blooms through the tangled grass,
As laughter ripples, let moments amass.

**Stories Traced in Delicate Green**

Underfoot, the fables grow,
In leafy lines, secrets flow.
A crinkled twig whispers sly,
As ants march in a determined tie.

Pinecone jesters juggle around,
With shades of laughter clothed in sound.
Frogs croak jokes in a hidden pond,
While turtles laugh, their shells respond.

A wildflower's wink gives a shout,
A cheeky breeze tosses clumsily about.
In tangled vines, quirks intertwine,
As nature's humor starts to shine.

## The Hidden Language of Woodland Life

In every nook, a chuckle hides,
Amongst the leaves, the fun abides.
A spider with a mustache so grand,
Weaves tales of mischief in silken strands.

Rustling bushes share a jest,
As shadows play at nature's behest.
A snail sliding down, slowest race,
While the fireflies twinkle, putting on a chase.

Beneath the bark, the puns abound,
Echoing laughter all around.
In the woodland's heart, joy takes flight,
A comedy show, in the soft twilight.

## Tangles of Heartstrings


In the garden where giggles grow,
The green dancers sway, quite a show.
Whispers of joy in the summer breeze,
Tickling my toes and teasing my knees.

With every twist, a chuckle flies,
A dance of green with funny ties.
Laughter echoes in leafy beds,
As mischief blooms in nature's spreads.

Fuzzy fronds tickle the shy,
They wink and wave, oh my, oh my!
Underneath the wild, wild sun,
Who knew nature could be such fun?

In this tangle of joyful glee,
I trip over roots, wild as can be.
With each leafy giggle, I find my way,
Through nature's pranks, I laugh all day.

## Echoes of the Forest Floor

Beneath the trees where shadows play,
The ground is a stage, come join the fray.
Squirrels chatter in a comic act,
While mushrooms sport hats, that's a fact!

Each rustle brings a quirky sound,
Echoes of laughter all around.
A snail sneezes, what a surprise!
With tiny giggles and wide-open eyes.

A parade of ants in a single file,
Marching on by with an awkward style.
They fumble and tumble with such great flair,
Making the woodland giggle in share.

The floor's a canvas, painted with fun,
Where shade and light dance under the sun.
So come take a stroll on this forest spree,
Where every step brings glee to thee.

## Silence Wrapped in Leaves

In a hush where whispers bloom,
Leaves wrapped around, dispelling gloom.
A soft rustle breaks the quiet air,
As nature giggles without a care.

Treetops chuckle, swaying light,
Casting shadows that playfully bite.
Each leaf a joke, each branch a quip,
In this comedic forest trip.

A critter peeks with a wink and grin,
Rolling on the ground, oh what a spin!
The breeze joins in with a subtle tease,
Tickling the branches and teasing the leaves.

Every nook hides a funny face,
A thoughtful thistle, an awkward space.
So stroll in silence, but hear the cheer,
For laughter's wrapped in leaves, my dear.

## The Language of Verdant Spirits


Communities formed where green things dwell,
Spirits of laughter casting a spell.
With giggles that sprout from the mossy clumps,
Teaching us joy with every little jump.

The chatty plants share jokes galore,
While the groundhogs laugh from their secret door.
A sarcastic tree with a bark so bold,
Tells tales of peace, or so I'm told.

The whispers of green hold secrets near,
Stories of joy, soaked in cheer.
In leaves, the jokes unfold and swirl,
With every gust, nature's joy unfurl.

So listen closely, let your heart be light,
Join the green in their playful flight.
With every step in this vibrant scene,
You'll find the jokes that nature's keen.

## **Heartbeats in Green**

In the forest where critters dance,
A leaf waved by chance,
They giggle and sway with delight,
Wonder what stirs in the night.

The sun tickles their fronds in glee,
Whispering secrets - can you see?
A snail slips by, wearing a hat,
Slyly thinking, 'Am I too fat?'

Bouncy mushrooms join the parade,
With polka dots that never fade,
A toad croaks, 'Let's start a band!'
A concert that's simply unplanned.

When evening falls, the mood gets high,
As shadows play tricks, oh my, oh my!
In giggles, the greens sway and twirl,
Creating chaos, a greenish whirl.

## The Fern's Secret Soliloquy

Amidst the greenery, secrets sprout,
Soft whispers echo, roundabout,
A dialogue held beneath the moon,
'Why can't we dance to a funny tune?'

Feeling bold with a tickling breeze,
They ponder with elegant unease,
A spider quips, 'I'm quite the star!'
As fireflies join from near and far.

Giggling leaves in a slow jam,
A hedgehog joins with a quick 'Wham!'
Swaying to the rhythm, oh what fun,
Under the gaze of the blushing sun.

The fronds weave tales of the bizarre,
Stirring up nature's nightly bazaar,
Laughter rings through the leafy green,
In this world, nothing's routine.

## Motions of the Heart in Moss

On a mossy stage where snails do glide,
The audience waits, hearts open wide,
Frogs in tuxedos with petals bright,
Anticipate laughter under the light.

A chubby hedgehog begins to groove,
With a shake that makes all hearts move,
The squirrels cheer with a nutty blast,
Hoping this wild affair will last.

Wiggling worms dig deep in the act,
Every wiggle a laugh, it's a fact,
In their muddy suits, they've come to play,
Mossy mayhem leads the way.

As dawn approaches, the dance slows down,
Leaves bow gracefully, wearing a crown,
Nature giggles, it's all just a game,
But the punchline's lost in the frond's name.

## Lush Dreams Ferned with Hope


In the wild woods, where dreams conspire,
Leaves whisper tales of a wild fire,
Shimmering hopes upon a wet leaf,
Bringing sunshine, despite all grief.

A chipmunk dreams in a flowery bed,
Afraid of what's lurking ahead,
But laughter bursts as he spots a friend,
Together they plot how to mend.

The dusk brings a light, winks through the trees,
A breeze laughs softly, tickling knees,
While all around, the greens conspire,
To keep spirits high and hearts afire.

Tomorrow will come, with new frolic and flair,
As foliage dances, we all must share,
For in this embrace of luck and play,
Life spins in circles, come what may.

## When Shadows Meet the Dappled Light

In the woods, a ticklish breeze,
Leaves laugh and shimmy with ease.
A squirrel prances, nuts in tow,
Tiptoeing softly, oh so slow.

Sunbeams dance on leafy greens,
Whispers hide in shaded scenes.
Campfire crackles, stories flow,
With shadows where the giggles grow.

Jokes float high on tufted beds,
While gnomes wear caps upon their heads.
A mushroom chuckles, round and stout,
As nature's antics swirl about.

In this place where whimsy reigns,
The wild and goofy break their chains.
A squirrel winks, a fox does grin,
In dappled light, let fun begin!

## A Canopy of Unspoken Thoughts

Beneath the leaves that nod and sway,
Secret laughs mingle with the play.
A spider spins a wily web,
While crickets chirp with a playful ebb.

A turtle pokes his nose out slow,
Is that a hat? No, just a crow!
The flowers giggle, colors bright,
As shadows twirl in sheer delight.

A worm in stripes shimmies along,
While butterflies sing a silly song.
The breeze, a rascal, tugs at hats,
Chasing dreams from furry chats.

In this realm of leafy glee,
Mirth and mischief roam so free.
A whispered joke, a snicker here,
Amidst the growth, let laughter cheer!

## Heartfelt Shadows Amongst the Stems

Glimmers of joy peek from the ground,
In the shade, giggles resound.
A dance of bumbles, all aglow,
Stirring sentiments beneath the show.

Dancing blades and mischief abound,
With unseen roots in laughter found.
The air is sweet with soft-spoken quips,
As nature shares her light-hearted tips.

In tangled greens where secrets lie,
A weary snail lets out a sigh.
"Life moves slow," he drowsily beams,
"Yet fun resides in sunlit dreams!"

From the shadows, a cackle breaks,
As rabbits wear their finest flakes.
With all the charm and jovial grace,
In this green nook, we find our place!

## Symbiosis of Emotion and Earth

Underneath the leafy layers,
Grins enchant like sunny prayers.
A dance of roots so intertwined,
Clever critters with jokes aligned.

Whispers flutter through the vines,
Where laughter spreads like secret signs.
Mossy beds of cuddly cheer,
Invite the frolics of all near.

Slugs in bow ties, what a sight!
And toads who croak out tunes at night.
As nature's giggles intertwine,
In this green realm, all is divine.

With every rustle, a chuckle grows,
In a world where whimsy flows.
So grab a friend for a leafy spree,
Amidst the fun of harmony!

## Soul Gardens of the Sylvan

In the woods where giggles sprout,
Plants sneak whispers, there's no doubt.
A squirrel chuckles at my shoe,
Dance with nature, join the crew.

Sunbeams flicker, shadows prance,
Foliage wiggles, join the dance.
Laughter echoes through the trees,
Nature's jokes are sure to please.

Mossy jokes and ferns that tease,
Every flower holds a gleeful breeze.
Petals may play, oh what a trick,
Beneath the canopies, time plays a flick.

So grab a leaf and take a seat,
Join the laughter, feel the beat.
In this garden, joy is free,
Oversized hats? It's the rule of three!

## **Whispers of Green Shadows**

Green whispers giggle between the leaves,
A gnome complains, 'Who's chewing my peas?'
The daisies gossip, 'Look at that ant!'
'He's trying to dance, but he can't!'

Bushes waltz, in breezy hijinks,
While squirrels bop to favorite jingles.
Clovers hide jokes that bloom like cheers,
Forget your worries, dismiss your fears.

A petunia's laugh rolls off a log,
As ivy wrestles with a playful frog.
'Hey, jump your way across this rock!'
Laughter echoes, you can't help but gawk.

So frolic through shadows, let joy abound,
Where nature's whispers make silly sounds.
In this green realm where giggles live,
It's the joy of nature that we give!

## Beneath the Canopy's Embrace

Under the canopy, the fun begins,
Where acorns tumble and giggling spins.
A badger's chuckle tickles my ears,
As bouncy ferns leap without fears.

Butterflies flutter in ridiculous styles,
Dancing around with the silliest smiles.
'Catch me if you can!' they tease and flit,
While the trees agree, 'A bit of wit!'

Caterpillars league on this leafy spree,
Discussing outrageous plans for tea.
The laughter branches, embracing the day,
As shadows encourage dousing the gray.

So bring your antics, let's stir up a storm,
In this leafy world, it's fun that we swarm.
Beneath the green sky, jokes take flight,
A mishmash of laughter, oh what a sight!

## Veils of Memories in the Breeze

Windy whispers twirl on a whimsied quest,
Breezy echoes and secrets jest.
A frond flips like it knows some news,
While dandelions dance in colorful shoes.

Petals drop like confetti that plays,
Nature's party, in bright sun rays.
'Tell me a joke!' the ivy implores,
While the toadstools 'round the laughter roars.

Memory sprouts in this lively space,
Where vines and greens form a cozy place.
Each giggle sown in the soil of cheer,
Will grow into smiles that linger near.

So let's frolic where humor is light,
In this quirky garden, a playful sight.
Veils of laughter, memories weave,
In the playtime realm where we believe!

## Fern-lined Paths of Personal Reflection

Along the trail, I trip and fall,
A clumsy dance, I heed the call.
The green confetti laughs and teases,
Nature's jury with no bad breezes.

In emerald robes, they wave goodbye,
As I stumble, they giggle, oh my!
My shoes are caked, my heart is light,
Who knew greens could cause such delight?

Lost in thought, I hear them whisper,
"Your fashion sense could use a crisper!"
These leafy pals, all wise and spry,
Give me sass as I slosh by.

Yet in their dance and vibrant cheer,
I find a joy that feels so near.
With every slip, I gain a grin,
In nature's laughter, I fit right in.

## **Intertwined Journeys in the Thicket**

In tangled roots, I make my way,
With furry friends who love to play.
They pull my leg, suggest a route,
Who knew that squirrels could be so cute?

Between the leaves, a riddle hides,
Where do I walk? My sense divides!
A playful gust gives me a shove,
The woodland shouts, 'You're made for love!'

As I navigate this leafy maze,
I swear I'm trapped in leafy craze.
But every twist grants laughs anew,
With leafy pals, there's much to view.

So let's twirl 'round in this green scene,
Chasing shadows, feeling keen.
With every hop, a cheerful song,
In nature's arms, I can't go wrong!

## **Whispers from the Heart in the Green**

With each step in the soft, damp clay,
The whispers tease, come out to play.
"Are you lost?", they gently poke,
Their jokes more subtle than a cloak.

The sun filters through a leafy screen,
Where laughter bubbles, sweet and clean.
"Don't mind the mud, just jump right in!,"
The vines around me start to grin.

A fern drops a wink, how bold!
In this wildness, my heart turns gold.
With roots entwined, I feel the thrill,
A love for laughter, nature's skill.

As shadows dance among the pines,
I laugh aloud, lose track of time.
In this lush world, I find my place,
With quirky greens, I join the race.

## The Forest's Embrace

In the forest where the wisps play,
I wander free, come what may.
The trees stand tall, they share a joke,
Their branches sway and softly poke.

A critter hops, just out of sight,
The forest chuckles with delight.
A squirrel shrieks, then takes a leap,
In this green realm where secrets seep.

Twisting trails, the paths unwind,
With every turn, a giggle behind.
I ask the ferns, "Do you agree?"
They nod their heads, oh what glee!

Amidst the leaves, I dance and twirl,
This lively place makes my heart whirl.
Enveloped here, I find my tune,
With nature's laugh beneath the moon.

## Shrouded in Tender Thought

In the underbrush, thoughts tumble down,
With leafy whispers, I wear a crown.
They tease my hair, my thoughts like blooms,
Comedic tangle, laughter looms.

A gentle breeze brings forth a jest,
"Chase that thought, it needs a rest!"
The dappled light beams down with flair,
As greenery grins, without a care.

In pools of shade, I ponder life,
The ferns shout, "No stress or strife!"
In their embrace, my worries fade,
A giggle here, a misstep made.

So let us revel in nature's heart,
With earthy humor as our art.
In tangled thoughts, I find my cheer,
Among these greens, I've nothing to fear.

## The Language of Green

In a world where leaves converse,
Whispers tickle my funny bone,
Tickled tongues of emerald hue,
Chirp and chatter, never alone.

A polka-dotted snail winks wide,
Sipping dew from a leaf's embrace,
With a smirk, he takes his ride,
Gliding through in leafy grace.

Sassier than a clover sprout,
A dandelion tells a joke,
Straight-faced blooms can never pout,
They chuckle 'til they choke and croak!

Laughter echoes through the glade,
Funky fungi join the fray,
In the shade, a jester played,
Where silly blooms come out to play.

## Secrets of the Shaded Grove

In the grove where shadows peek,
A mischievous breeze takes flight,
It passes leaves with a cheeky squeak,
Teaching roots to dance at night.

A squirrel spins tales of glory,
With acorns as his treasure chest,
He spins the forest's wild story,
Squeaking laughter, never stressed.

The wise old tree is not so meek,
With knots and gnarls, he barks a pun,
"Why don't you ever hear them speak?
Because their roots just want to run!"

Beneath the branches, secrets shine,
Bubbly laughter, the leaves applaud,
Nature's best comic design,
Making even the serious nod.

## **Lush Lamentations**

In a patch where greens collide,
A cabbage starts a silly fight,
With lettuce taking a proud stride,
Claiming he's the veggie knight!

The spinach rolls its leafy eyes,
"Who needs armor when you're fresh?"
With broccoli, their laughter flies,
"Let's have a squabble, enmesh!"

But in this garden of delight,
Petunias chuckle, petals sway,
"We'll settle this with a pillow fight!"
As rainclouds grin and drift away.

So come and join the veggie brawl,
Where raucous laughter fills the air,
In this lush lament, we all enthrall,
Nature's jesters without a care!

## **Breezes through the Fernvale**

Through the vale, a tangle plays,
Where the wind whispers cheeky tales,
It tickles leaves in sunny rays,
While giggles swirl like tiny trails.

A shaggy dog in leafy shade,
Wags his tail, a playful sight,
With a bounce, he leapt and stayed,
Chasing shadows in the light.

The daisies join in with a cheer,
"Let's twirl and swirl, don't be shy!"
As butterflies flit without fear,
Flapping wings that wave goodbye.

In the heart of this joyful glen,
Where breezes dance and spirits lift,
Nature's laughter comes again,
In the ferny world, the best gift!

www.ingramcontent.com/pod-product-compliance
Lightning Source LLC
Chambersburg PA
CBHW050611100526
44585CB00034B/1452